Tragic setbacks and bounce back

Table of contents

C bounces back

D. everything will change for the better or worse?

I suffered too many unfair setbacks in my life. The challenges are too many but somehow I got the strength to continue to go for the dreams despite the obstacles.

A.Overcoming obstacles

I came into this world with too many obstacles. I was

born to chaos,
violence, and
the curse of
bad people
being
interested in

me and
wanting to hurt
me.I cannot let
these people
stop me. I
cannot be with

badpeople, despair, criminals, and evildoers. Bad grades and misfortunes. A music career that never got off the ground. Most importantly, I was never loved, or accepted in this American society I live in. Regardless, the only way for

me to believe
in something
better than the
limited reality is
to continue to
dream and

make an effort.
I do believe
that everything
will get better.
I really do
because I

cannot live with

evil people, I

cannot become

an evil person.

Regardless

because of my

skin color,
unique
personality and
my ambitions, I
keep attracting
the wrong

people- the criminals, the users, the dream killers who want to steal my home ,

my songs, take
away my
dreams ,
destroy me for
the wrong
reasons and

this is something I cannot let them do .

Hang in there, overcome

B. Unfair Suffering

I have a unique personality, I am an artist but this artistry and

the use of my
intellect had
forced me to
see too much
suffering in my
life and of

others. In this world, there is just too much tragedy and chaos to truly understand it.

The world is skewed with superficiality, power struggles and there is enough crime to know that

the power of

love and

salvation as

well as

happiness in

not outside of
the self, myself.
It is within
myself,
yourself, the
truth is, is I love

myself, then I

can love

someone else.

For me ,it is

hard to love or

feel loved when

I wake up in the morning and I go outside and hear the catcalls, the name calling outside my window, the news of gossip and cruelty that is in man inhumanity to man . This same energy is directed at me ,and since I was born, I was subjected to

bullies,- danger
is in sight for
someone else
to put me
down , call me
names,

prejudge me

constantly

which is an evil

I live with since,

This is unfair

suffering but I

got to believe
that there is a
better
tomorrow ,and
that is the only
way ,or the

alternative is to give up.

C. bounces
back

Mental illness
and crime has
been a curse I
had to deal

with it from others since I was a kid. From being beaten for no reason constantly as a child ,to as an adult ,hearing a deranged person stalking me and thinking I am

mentally
retarded due
their delusions
on me and
those who do
not want me to

succeed or
know common
sense yet this
sickness is a
part of hell
which is on

earth. I do believe that things will get better and they will and so should you?

Life is within for me and writing about it is enough to keep me going.

D. everything will change for the better or worse?

I really do believe things will get better because nothing stays the same and everything will change, for the better. For us all, no matter where you come from

because we
are one but we
are not the
same
personality but
we are the

same human
species ,black
white or brown
,we got to carry
each other

www.ingramcontent.com/pod-product-compliance
Lightning Source LLC
Chambersburg PA
CBHW050348290526
45785CB00006B/2679